Celtic Cittern
by Doc Rossi

An Approach to Playing
Traditional Dance Music
on the Cittern

T0070628

ISBN 978-1-57424-261-4
SAN 683-8022

Cover by James Creative Group

Copyright © 2010 CENTERSTREAM Publishing, LLC
P.O. Box 17878 - Anaheim Hills, CA 92817

www.centerstream-usa.com

All rights for publication and distribution are reserved.
No part of this book may be reproduced in any form or by any Electronic or mechanical mtans including information storage and retrieval systems
without permission in writing from the publisher, except by reviewers who may quote brief passages in review.

This book is dedicated to the traditional musicians who have helped me learn to play their music - Lucy Farr, Tommy Healy, Jimmy Power, Bob Cann, Dan Quinn, Roger Digby, and The Rakes: Paul Gross, Michael Plunkett and Reg Hall.

Thanks to Peter Abnett, Pedro Caldeira Cabral, Ugo Casalonga, Ian Chisholm, Damien Delgrossi, Paul Doyle, Andy Irvine, Mathieu Luzi, Christian Magdeleine, Ale Möller, Malcolm Prior, Martina Rosenberger and Joseph Sobol.

All photographs by Adrian Frearson

CONTENTS

INTRODUCTION

If you look through the titles of the tunes in this book, you'll see that most of them come from Irish traditional music. Irish music has had an enormous influence on the revival of traditional musics of Western cultures, thanks to pioneering groups like The Chieftains, Planxty, The Bothy Band, De Dannan, and a host of others. The energy and drive of Irish traditional music and the success of popular bands who have brought it to a wider audience has inspired musicians from other countries and cultures to take the traditional music of their own culture to a different level. A prime example is Alan Stivell, who spearheaded a revival of Breton music with his *Renaissance of the Celtic Harp*. Another is Ale Möller and his work with Scandinavian traditional music. Today we can enjoy a variety of "Celtic" music from all over Europe because "Celtic" has become a style or aesthetic approach as much as anything else.

I concentrate on Irish tunes in this book because Irish traditional music is so well known and appreciated, and also because it has a highly evolved style of ornamentation and variation. I've also included some tunes from other countries and cultures not just because they're great tunes, but to help you understand how what you learn in one style of music can be carried over into another without blurring the differences into some nondescript mix. What I'm working on is a style of playing the cittern that respects the traditions that the music comes from while making the most of the idiomatic characteristics of the cittern itself.

Although the cittern is not (yet) a traditional instrument in Irish music, it is the traditional instrument *par excellence* in Portugal, where it is known as the *guitarra*, and in Corsica, where it is called the *cetera*. Since the middle 1970s there has been a bewildering variety of names and specifications for citterns, bouzoukis, octave mandolins, mandolas and mandocellos. Cittern is a family of instruments that includes all of these instruments, and it is also an instrument within that family. Historically, the cittern has had anywhere from 4 to 14 sets or courses of strings, a variety of tunings, a variety of shapes and sizes, and a vibrating string length ranging from shorter than a mandolin (photo on page 71) to slightly longer than that of a modern guitar.

The cittern does have a historical link to traditional music that goes back to the middle of the 18th century when the so-called English *guittar* or *cetra* was a popular instrument for domestic music making throughout most of Western Europe. Publications for this instrument feature jigs, slip jigs, reels and hornpipes, some of which are still played today. The music published by John Playford is not strictly traditional even though many of the tunes are still used for dancing. Playford published at least three cittern books in the 17th century that are full of such dances. In fact, the story of how the modern cittern came to be is linked to the older instruments.

The Portuguese *guitarra*, Coriscan *cetera*, Swiss *halszither* and German *waldzither* are modern citterns in that they have survived until today, while the Irish bouzouki and the modern cittern were invented in the 1960s and 70s (but see the photo on page 25). Portuguese legend Carlos Paredes commissioned a long-scale version of the *guitarra* in the 1960s, but it didn't catch on. Johnny Moynihan is credited with introducing the Greek bouzouki to Irish traditional music, while Andy Irvine used the *guitarra* and the *waldzither* as well as the bouzouki and mandolin. Johnny Moynihan had a flat-backed bouzouki in the mid- to late-60s that had been built by John Bailey for guitarist John Pearse. It was based on the English *guittar* and Portuguese *guitarra* body with a bouzouki neck. A little later, when Dónal Lunny wanted a flat-backed bouzouki with unison rather than octave pairs of strings, he went to English luthier Peter Abnett who invented the Irish bouzouki for him, and the modern cittern family was truly born. Peter's instruments have a three-piece dished back to preserve the characteristic sound of the Greek bouzouki, but use the cittern shape, bridge and tailpiece. Peter had experience of early instruments and so knew about earlier citterns. Today he calls his 5-course, shorter scale instruments citterns.

A few years after Peter Abnett had invented the Irish bouzouki and Planxty had made it world famous, Stefan Sobell, who was not yet a full-time builder, made himself a 4-course, carved-top, pear-shaped instrument that he called a cittern. He had also been influenced by early instruments, especially the English *guittar*, the Portuguese *guitarra* and the renaissance cittern. He tends to call his long-scale instruments bouzoukis, his shorter ones citterns regardless of the number of courses. These days there are hundreds of builders and variations on the venerable cittern design. Unfortunately, that first bouzouki that started the modern revival - the one Peter Abnett built for Dónal Lunny - was destroyed in a fire.

Using This Book

This book is designed for a 5-course instrument, with whatever vibrating string length that suits you. The tuning used is G D A D G - like the Irish bouzouki with an extra course on top. With its similarity to fiddle and banjo tuning plus fourths on the top, G D A D G makes it easy to play tunes in all the important traditional keys or modes without using a capo or having to negotiate difficult position shifts, while at the same time providing a number of open strings and other possibilities for playing your own accompaniments. It is also a good tuning for playing chords, bass lines and counter-melodies. You can tune to whatever actual pitches you like or that suit the string length of your instrument as long as you maintain the intervals of a fifth, a fifth, a fourth and a fourth, from the lowest note to the highest (a fifth is seven frets; a fourth is five). For example, on a guitar-size instrument, you might tune down a whole step to F C G C F and capo at the second fret. In fact, guitarists can play from the tablature using those pitches and tuning the sixth string down to C for an extra drone. In addition to tablature, I've included notation for anyone who would like to play these tunes in a different tuning. The notation doesn't include left-hand fingerings, but it does include all of the ornaments.

This book is primarily about melody playing, so I don't talk about accompaniment beyond including some very basic chords. Traditional music is often drone-based and modal rather than based on a system of major and minor keys, so there are not a lot of basic chord progressions that fit several tunes. It is my feeling that to play good backup you have to know the tunes, so take this book as a first step - learn the tunes, then learn to accompany them. Basic chord shapes are given in the appendix, but I don't want to encourage banging out the chords behind the tunes! Accompaniment is a very subtle art. The most important advice I can give about backing up is listen to whom you're playing with and don't swamp them.

The tablature follows normal conventions: the top line represents the top or highest-pitched course; the lower represents the fifth or lowest course; numbers represent frets, with 0 being an open string. The rhythm markings are the same as those used in standard guitar notation, meaning that it is slightly simplified to make it easier to read, and so you should let some notes ring on longer than indicated. A tie or slur between notes of different pitches indicates that the first note is sounded with the pick, with the note or notes following being hammer-ons, pull-offs or slides. Some slides are also marked with an S. I haven't marked the places where I bend one note into another. I often do this when going from a fretted note to an open one, for example, from f# on the second course to the top g. Two parallel slashes in the final measure of a tune means that the tune ends on the note just before them. Grace notes are smaller than main notes and can be left out when you are first learning a tune. Part One uses two staffs to illustrate the basics of ornamentation, with a basic version of the tune in the top staff and a decorated version below. In the rest of the book, ornamentation and variations are indicated by lower-case letters above the measure that refer to the alternate measures at the end of the piece. The last three pieces in the book are duets for two citterns.

PART ONE - Basic Technique & Ornamentation

I use a rather stiff yet thin flatpick - a Tortex .60 (orange) - and I use the rounded edge rather than the point. I find this gives me a fuller tone and that the pick glides over the strings more easily. I adjust my grip as required to make the flatpick more or less flexible. I try to keep my right wrist as loose as possible and in general use an up-and-down motion, except when playing jigs, which are discussed later. My right arm comes more around the end of the cittern rather than over the top like a guitarist would do. I rest my free right-hand fingers very lightly on the top of the cittern. I also occasionally rest my wrist or forearm on the bridge, but in general I try to keep my wrist as free as possible.

For the left hand, the second fret is "home" - that is, the index finger hovers over the second fret, going down to the first only when necessary. The middle, ring and little finger cover frets three, four and five respectively, but I often find that I want to use a stronger finger on the fourth or fifth fret, especially when there is an ornament involved, so I move my left hand up the neck and fret with the middle or ring finger - whatever feels most comfortable and solid.

Traditional music is primarily oral, but many traditional players do take tunes from tune books. Most printed sources give rather bare settings of the tunes with little or no ornamentation indicated, and it is up to the players to bring them to life and make them their own. In this first section we look at the basic ornaments as they might be played in some well-known tunes. All of the ornamentation in this section is written out in full in the lower staff. In Part Two and Part Three, several ornaments are included in the tab, while others are given at the end of the piece in alternate measures. Ornamentation in traditional music is improvised and spontaneous. I try to show you which ornaments might be played where, but these arrangements are not written in stone: they are simply my take on it based on what I've learned from the musicians who taught me.

Ornamentation and variation are very important in Irish traditional music, and each instrument has its own idiomatic ornaments. Since the cittern is a relative newcomer, the door is open for us to discover which ornaments suit it best, but we can and should learn from traditional players on other instruments. The obvious choice might be the banjo, and a lot can be learned from traditional banjo players, but the banjo and the cittern are also very different in terms of attack, sustain, tone, tension and stringing. It is important to listen to all of the main traditional instruments to understand the intricacies of ornamentation and variation, then apply what you learn to the cittern.

Most ornaments on the cittern are played using hammer-ons, pull-offs, or slides. They should be played quickly, without putting the other notes in the bar out of time. In other words, they "borrow" time from the notes near them. Don't dwell too long on the ornaments - they are really just a flick of a left-hand finger or two and should add bounce and lightness. The exception to this is the plucked triplet, which is primarily a right-hand ornament. They should also be played light and bouncy; they sometimes have a more percussive rather than melodic effect. Here is a brief rundown of what the ornaments look like on paper. You can hear them in context on the CD.

A single grace note or *acciaccatura* is written as a small eighth note with a line through its stem. They are often placed between notes of the same pitch, or before an important note to give it more emphasis. Pick the grace and pull off for the main note.

Double grace notes or trills are written as two sixteenth notes. Pick the first note, then quickly hammer-on and pull-off the next two.

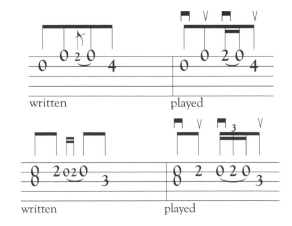

Triplets are three notes played in the place of two. There are several kinds - plucked, slurred, ascending and descending. They are often shown in tune books, but are also used to decorate quarter notes or to fill in between notes that are more than a step apart.

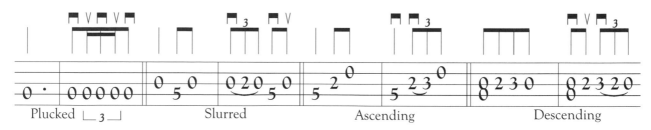

Rolls or turns are four- or five-note ornaments that use the notes just above and below the main note. Often played as triplets on plucked instruments, they are used to decorate quarter notes and dotted quarter notes, or a group of quarter and eighth notes of the same pitch.

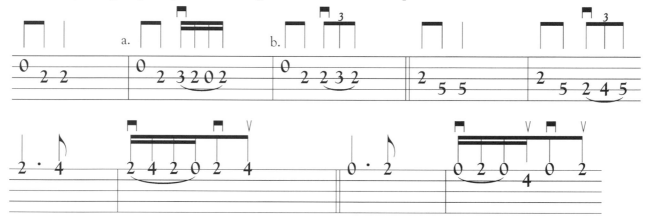

Cranning or popping is a technique used by pipers on the low D or E. It is played by lifting off single fingers in quick succession to achieve a bubbling effect. We can imitate this on the cittern using a quick succession of a hammer-on and two pull-offs.

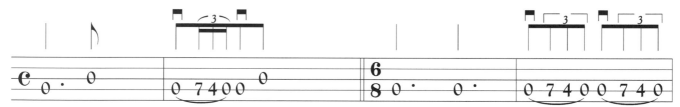

The cittern has a lot of sustain, so a note ringing on without any added ornamentation can be very effective, as can adding harmony notes or chords. Keep in mind that ornamentation can be overdone. Silence and space are often overlooked elements of tasteful playing.

We start off with The Peacock's Feather and The Fairies' Hornpipe. The Fairies' is made up of three strands - measures 1-4, 5-8 and 9-12. Measures 13-16 are the same as 5-8, but note the descending triplet in measure 15 - this is a typical ornament or variation. The Peacock's Feather has a similar structure and several descending triplets.

The Long Note may be the only tune whose name actually describes a musical characteristic of the tune itself. The variations in the second staff show several ways of playing dotted quarter notes. These would normally be rolled except that the main note is the low open D where a real roll isn't possible, so instead I use sliding into a unison, hammering on to a unison, plucked triplets, and a cran. Other ornaments in this setting include triplets and rolls replacing quarter notes, plus single and double graces.

The Peacock's Feather

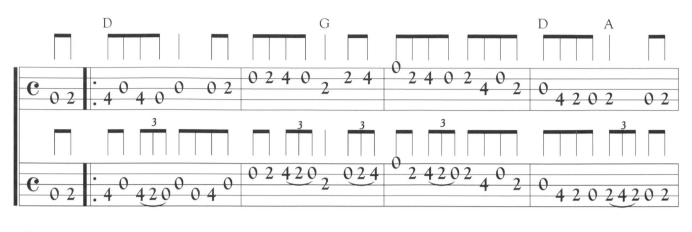

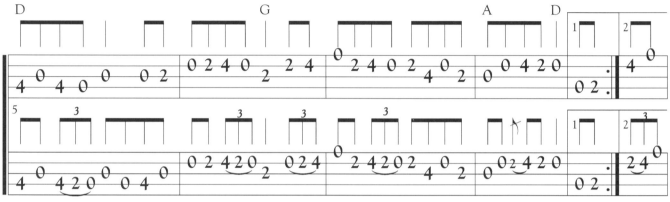

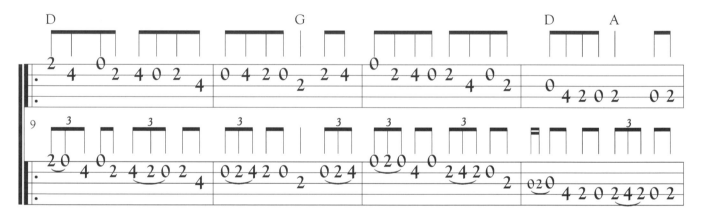

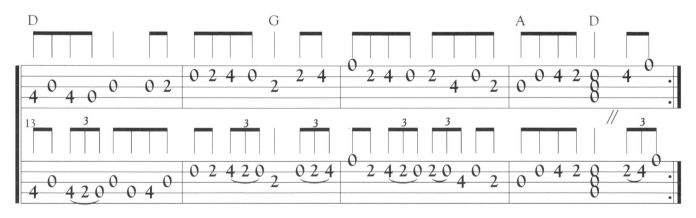

© 2010 Gregory Doc Rossi

The Fairies' Hornpipe

© 2010 Gregory Doc Rossi

The Long Note

© 2010 Gregory Doc Rossi

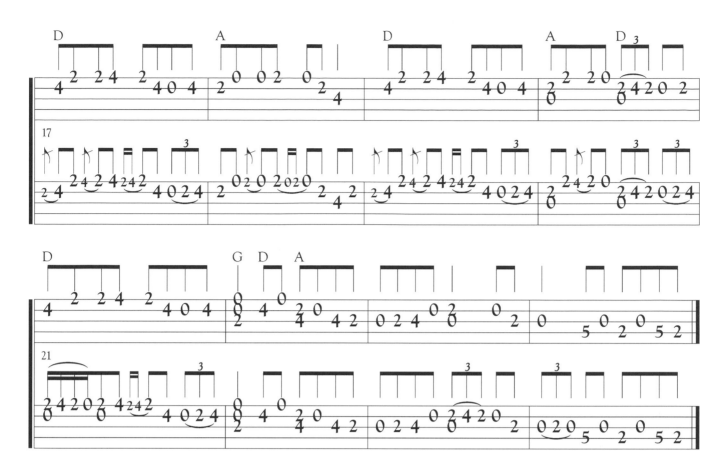

Two jigs coming up. There are different ways to pick jigs; the two most common I've seen traditional banjo players use are down-up-down/down-up-down and down-up-down/up-down-up, with string crossings sometimes breaking the pattern. I favor the first pattern because I like the drive it naturally has, but it does have the awkward feature of consecutive downstrokes, which can sometimes be tricky in quick tunes. In addition to adding more drive and interest, ornaments can also make a tricky passage easier to play by breaking the pattern while retaining the natural accents downstrokes give. This is often done with triplets, which in jigs look like this:

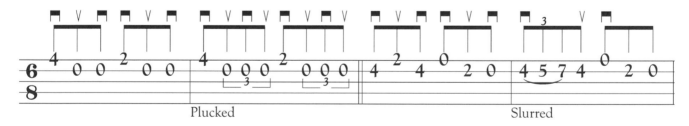

I learned The Humours of Kilcogher from piper and pipe maker Didier Heuline; my arrangement uses plucked triplets in several measures, crans in measures 3 and 4, and a harmonic variation in measures 11-12 which I play the last time through. I learned The Cordal Jig from The Rakes - Reg Hall (melodeon and piano), Michael Plunket (fiddle and flute) and Paul Gross (fiddle and piano), who were often joined by Ron Somers (drums), Lucy Farr (fiddle) and Tommy Healy (flute). The Cordal Jig, or Julia Clifford's, shows different ways of playing a dotted quarter note in measures 1, 5 and 17. The quarter notes throughout the tune can be played as trills, rolls or triplets; the one in measure 7 is perfect for an ascending triplet. Measures 2 and 15 show typical variations.

I learned Rodney's Glory - a set dance that is often played as a hornpipe or reel - from Martin Byrnes's excellent Leader LP. He uses a lot of ornamentation in his elegant, lilting style.

The Humours of Kilcogher

© 2010 Gregory Doc Rossi

12

The Cordal Jig

© 2010 Gregory Doc Rossi

13

Rodney's Glory

© 2010 Gregory Doc Rossi

PART Two - A Selection of Irish Tunes

Jigs

Brian O'Lynn is another fine, driving tune from Martin Byrnes. Note the single graces on the first notes of measures 1, 3, 5, 7 and 15, and the triplets in the alternate measures at the end. A Trip to Athlone and The Mist Covered Mountain are popular session tunes. They have several instances of plucked triplets, as well as several single graces.

The Mooncoin is a three-part jig in A mixolydian, easy enough to play if not taken too quickly. Note measures 1 and 5, and 9 and 13 - I use plucked triplets to break up the standard picking pattern, effectively avoiding consecutive downstrokes. There are also plenty of single graces between consecutive notes of the same pitch.

The Lark in the Morning is a popular four-part jig in D. As with The Mooncoin, there are plenty of plucked triplets and single graces. I've written out alternative endings which can be substituted for any of the others: a single grace note in measure 16 and a plucked triplet in measure 24. I don't necessarily play this as written - these are just some ideas for you to try.

Brian O'Lynn

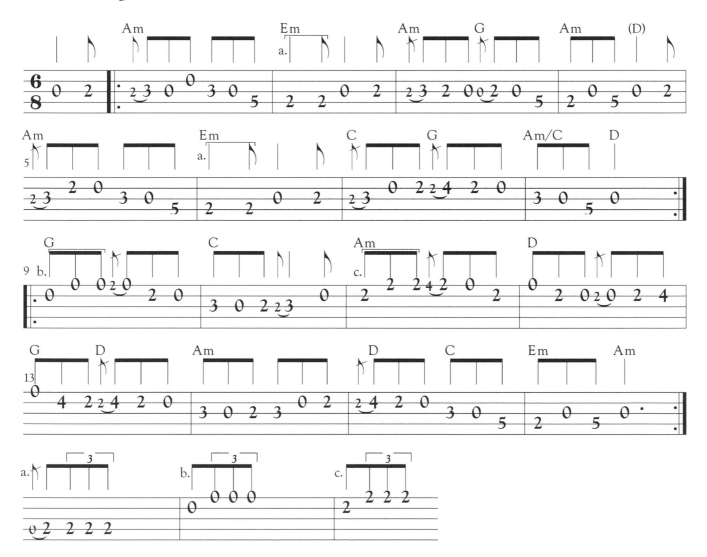

© 2010 Gregory Doc Rossi

A Trip to Athlone

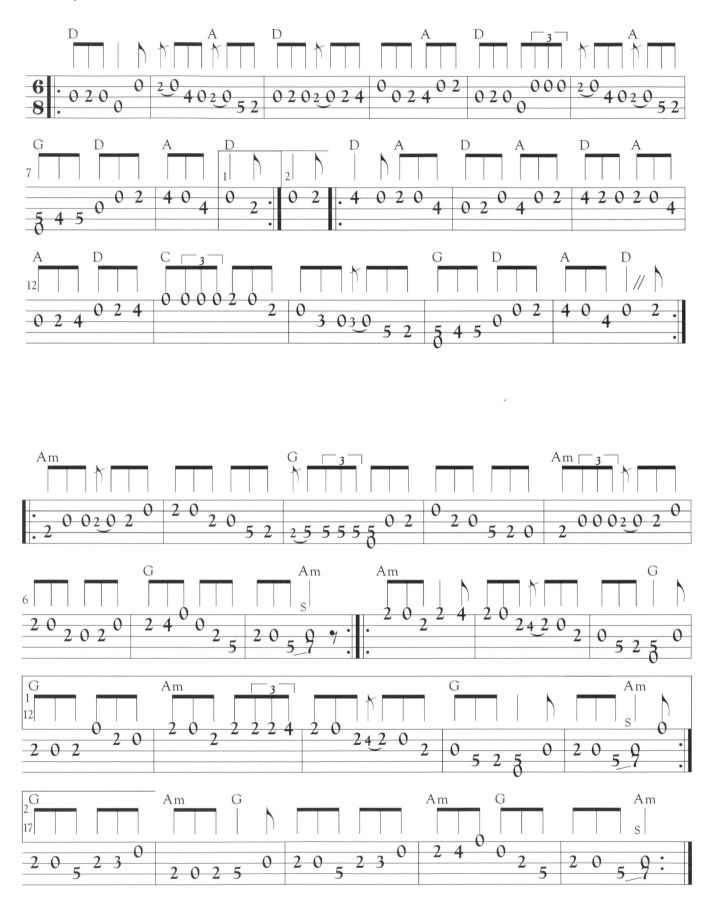

© 2010 Gregory Doc Rossi

16

The Mooncoin Jig

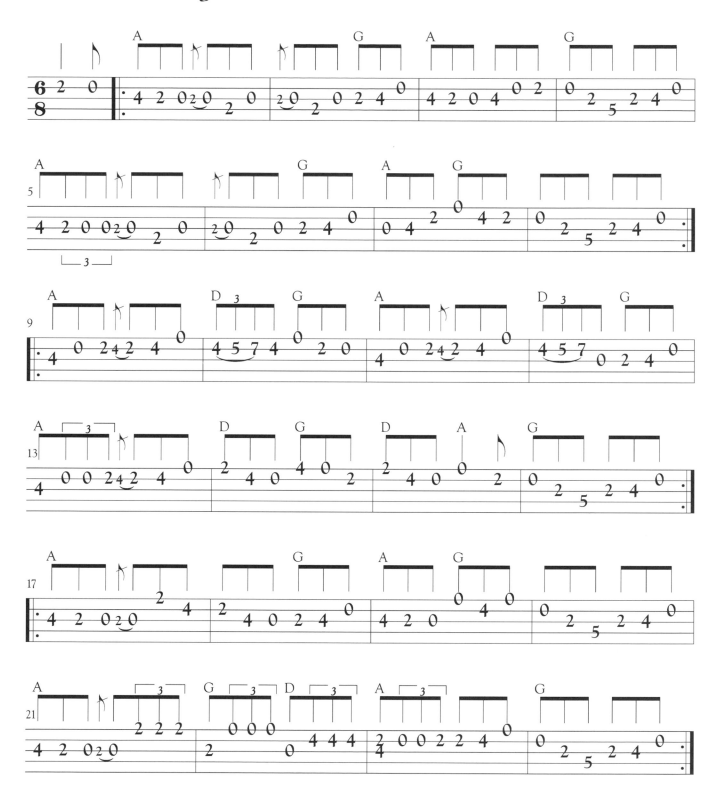

© 2010 Gregory Doc Rossi

The Lark in the Morning

© 2010 Gregory Doc Rossi

An Phis Fhliuch is a classic slip jig from the piping of Willy Clancy. Slip jigs and hop jigs are in 9/8 time - three beats per measure with the dotted quarter having one beat. I learned this tune off one of Willy Clancy's Topic recordings and have tried to adapt some of his ornaments and variations to the cittern.

The Swallow Tail is a popular session tune in Em. Its chief difficulty is barring across two or three courses to maintain a drone on E. The Banks of Lough Gowna is in Bm. There are several ways of ornamenting the repeated notes in measures 1 and 5 and the dotted quarters in measures 9 and 13.

An Phis Fhliuch

© 2010 Gregory Doc Rossi

The Swallow Tail Jig

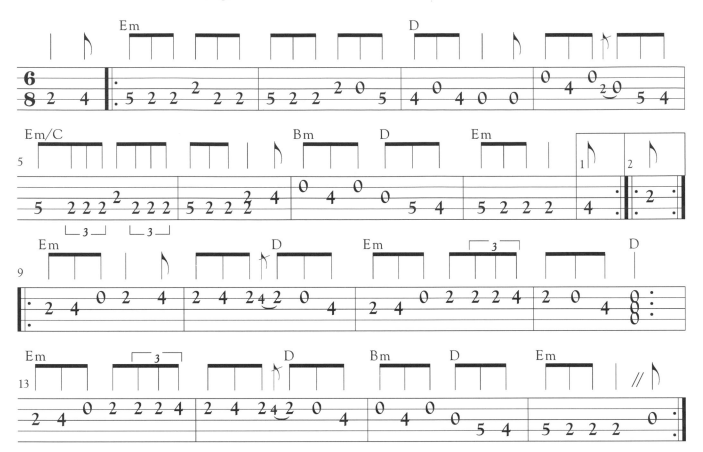

The Banks of Lough Gowna

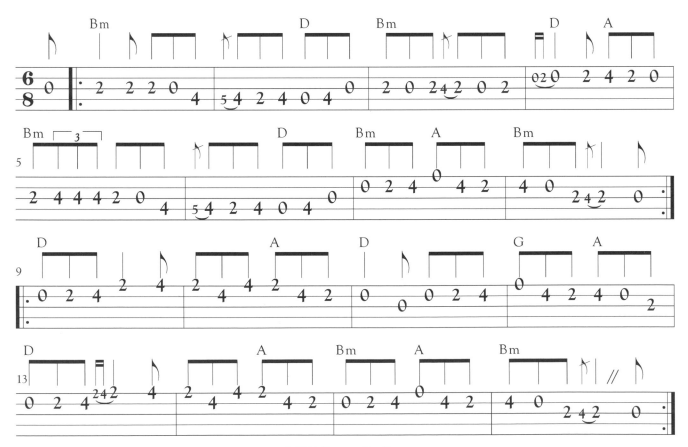

© 2010 Gregory Doc Rossi

Hornpipes & Set Dances

Poll Ha'penny dates from at least the 18th century. Apparently Turlough O'Carolan liked this tune so much that he said he would rather have written it more than any of his own tunes.

Poll Ha'penny

© 2010 Gregory Doc Rossi

I learned The Cliff and The Galway from Reg Hall, who plays them on the G/D melodeon. Ornaments in The Cliff include a triplet in measure 8, and a descending triplet in measure 16. Notice that the first half of measures 10 and 11 are the same except that the latter includes a descending triplet. Reg plays measures 1 and 5 as in the variation, but other versions have the D on the third beat, which is easier to play, especially when you're starting out. I've included more ornaments in the alternate version of measures 9-12. There are similar variations for The Galway, including two ways of decorating a middle G (variations a and b), and two ways to add triplets. To play the triplet in b, I slide the index finger up to the fourth fret.

The Cliff

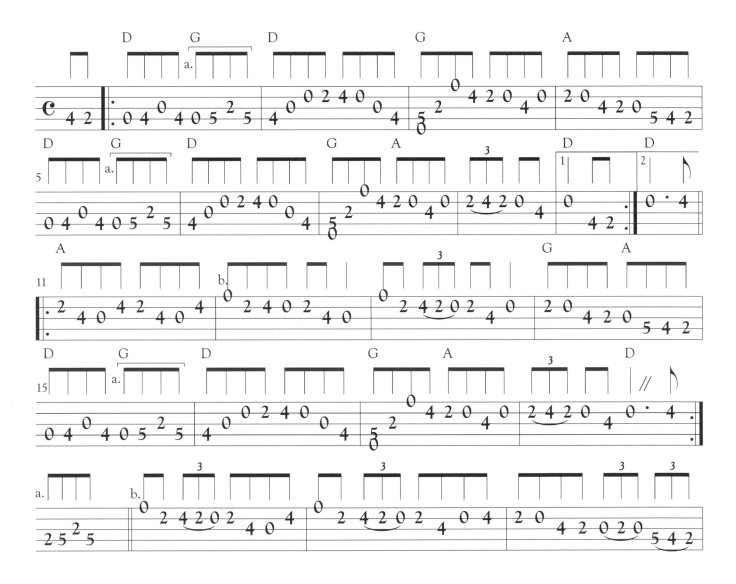

© 2010 Gregory Doc Rossi

The Galway

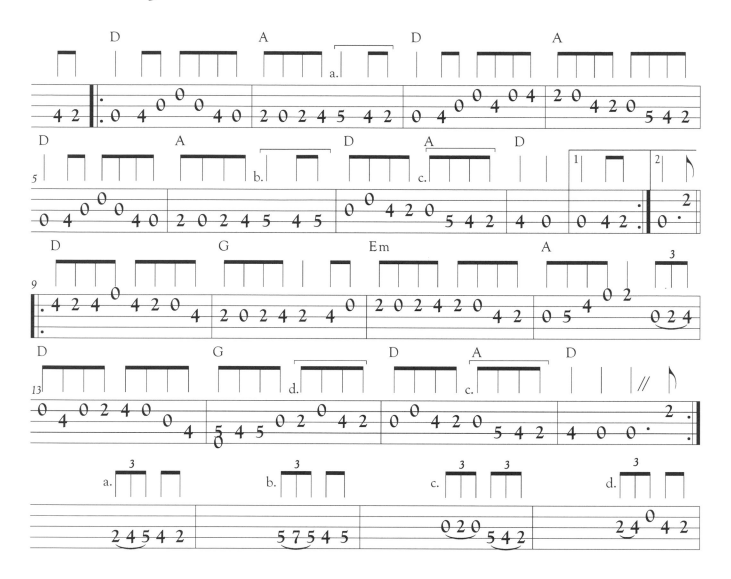

The Rakes in 1986. Clockwise from left, Michael Plunkett,
Ron Somers, Reg Hall, Hugh Rippon (caller), Paul Gross,
Lucy Farr, Tommy Healy.

I learned the Greencastle and Liverpool hornpipes from the great concertina player Roger Digby. Roger plays the Greencastle as given here, and I've included an alternate B part that I've heard others play. This tune is played as often in D as it is in G. In the Liverpool, the last four measures of each part are the same, so the B part shows variations you can use, while the recording demonstrates others.

The Greencastle Hornpipe

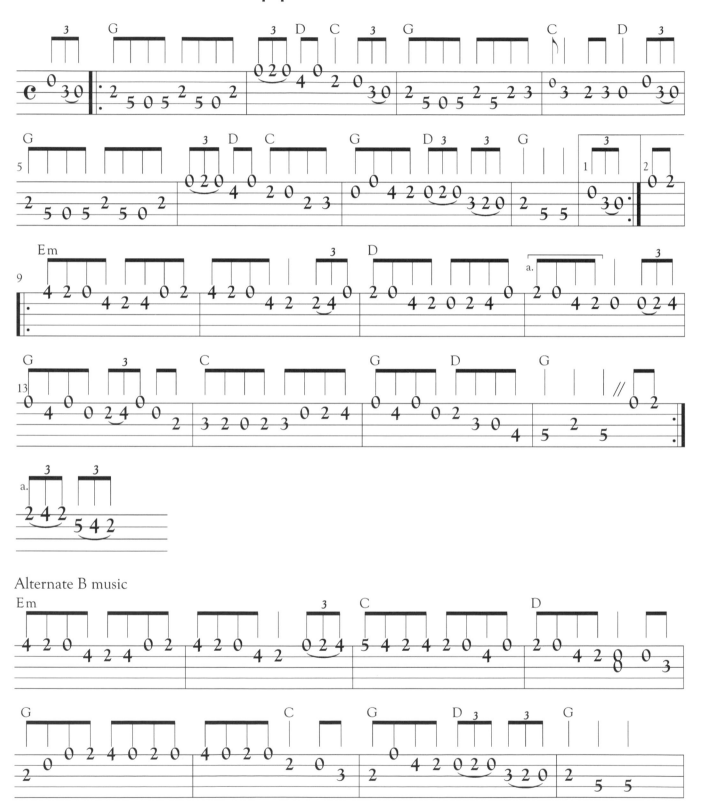

Alternate B music

© 2010 Gregory Doc Rossi

The Liverpool Hornpipe

The first version of The Princess Royal (measures 1-20) is often attributed to O'Carolan. I learned the other version from Michael Plunkett and Paul Gross of The Rakes; they in turn had it from two of the McCusker brothers, who recorded it live for the BBC on unison fiddles. My arrangement of the Blackbird is based on Martin Byrnes' setting. He played it with Rodney's Glory.

The first Celtic cittern?
A French postcard from the early 1900s.

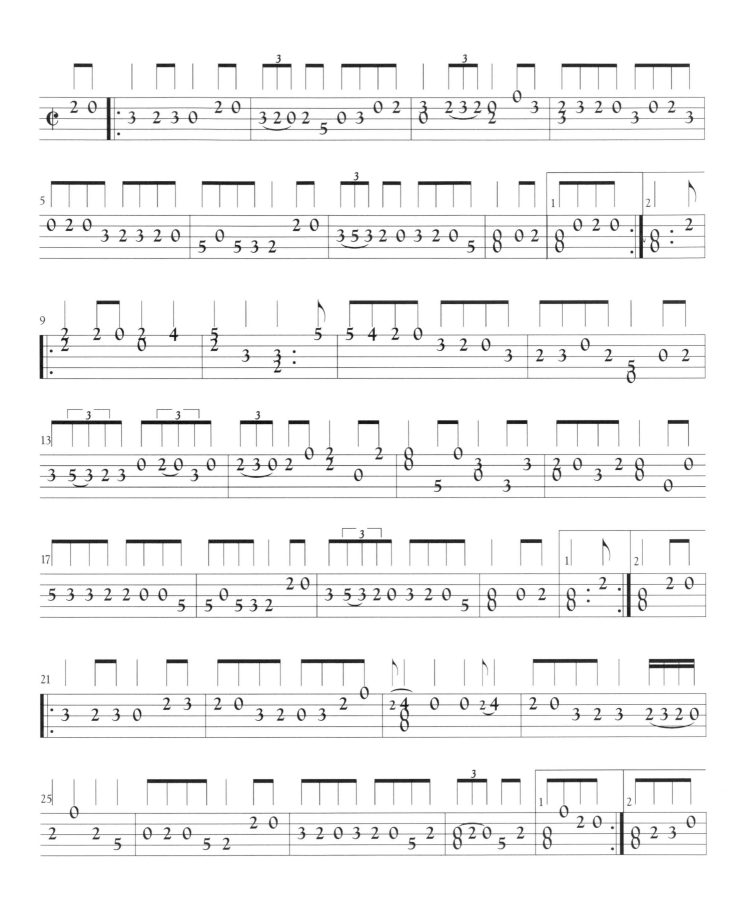

© 2010 Gregory Doc Rossi

The Blackbird

© 2010 Gregory Doc Rossi

28

The Flowers of Edinburgh is very well known as both a hornpipe and a reel. The Flowers of Michigan is a rare tune with some similarities to the Jug of Punch and The Temperance Reel, which Tommy Healy and I used to play together whenever we had the chance.

The only recording I've heard of this version of The Woman of the House is by De Danann, which they play with The Log Cabin, a great reel that has been recorded many times. I learned The Virginia from The Rakes.

The final medley of reels comes from The McCusker brothers, a nine-piece ceildh band that recorded them at break neck speed back in the 1950s. I think The Traveler's shows just how useful the top G course can be - I bounce off of it quite a lot in this tune and in Miss Thorton's. It helps me build up the momentum and lets me syncopate things a bit more easily. I give an alternative way of playing the B part of Miss Thorton's that gives a more open sound. I also give an alternate B part for The Scholar that is not traditional. The usual chords here would be D and C, but moving the lower line down chromatically adds a different dimension to the tune the second time around.

The Flowers of Edinburgh

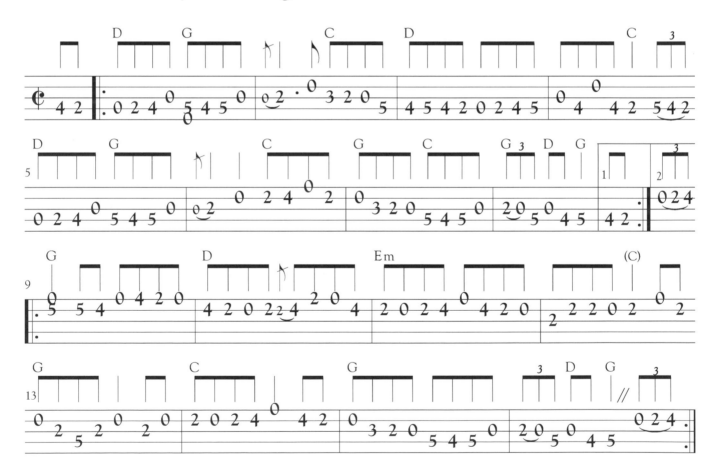

© 2010 Gregory Doc Rossi

The Flowers of Michigan

The Temperance

The Woman of the House

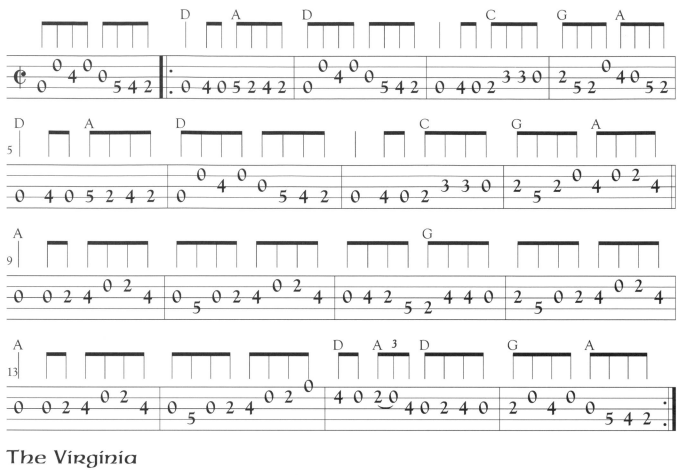

The Virginia

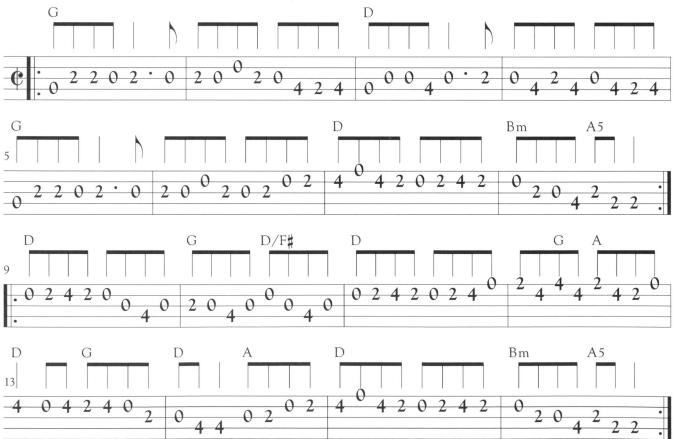

© 2010 Gregory Doc Rossi

The Log Cabin

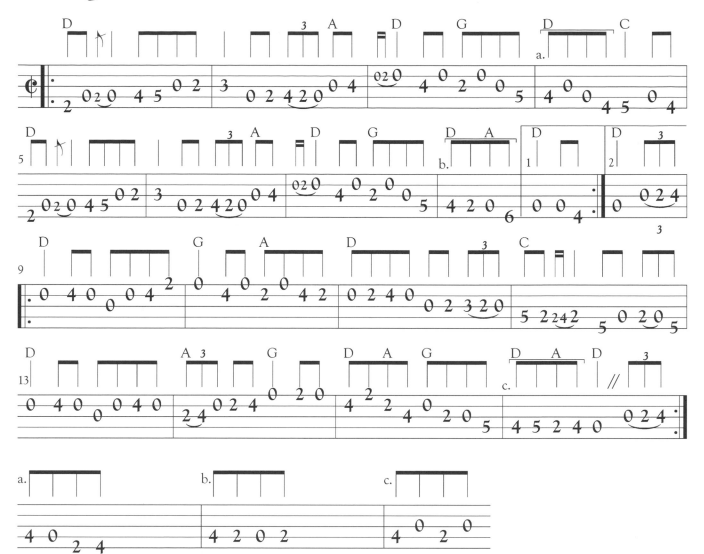

My Peter Abnett cittern
(left) and my Ian Chisholm
baritone cittern.

The Traveler's

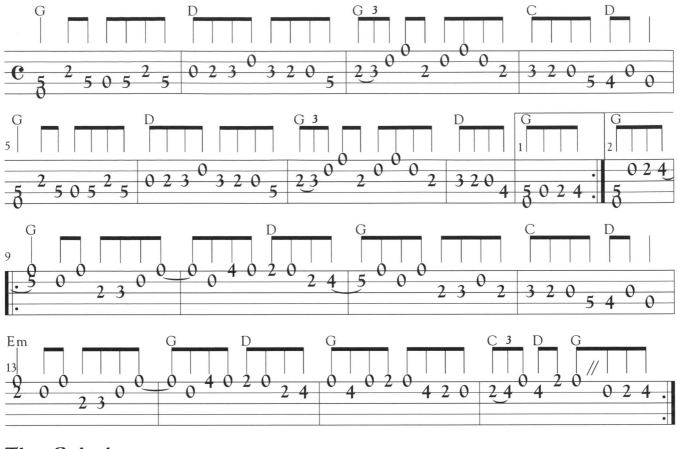

The Scholar

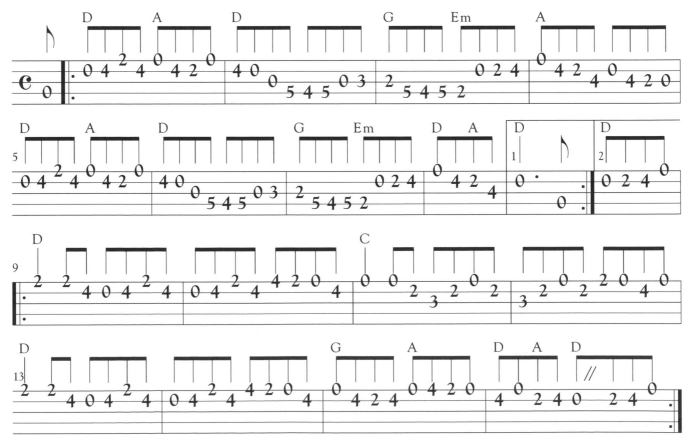

© 2010 Gregory Doc Rossi

Alternate B music

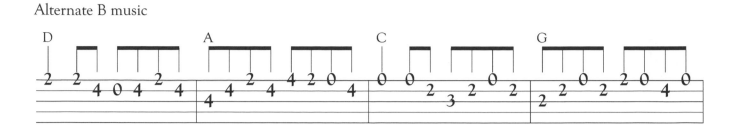

Miss Thorton's

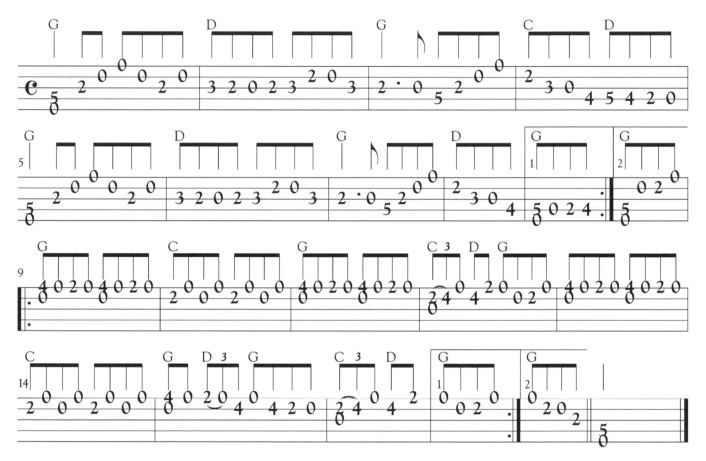

Alternate fingering for B music

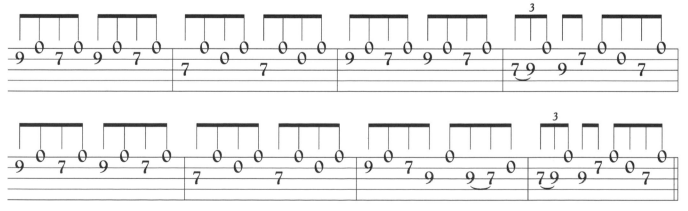

© 2010 Gregory Doc Rossi

PART Three - Tunes from other Cultures

American Old Time music owes a lot to Irish and Scottish music, but has a character all its own. I learned this version of Polly Put the Kettle On from banjo player David Murphy. I play it with a lot of swing and let the drones ring as much as possible.

I first heard French-Canadian music through recordings of Louis Beaudoin and of the Richlieu family. There is a tradition of playing what they call crooked tunes, or tunes with an uneven number of measures and/or unexpected phrasing, just to keep the dancers alert. Although usually played as a single tune, this piece is actually made up of two tunes - La Cardeuse and Le Triomphe. There have been several recordings of them with the parts arranged in different ways. I like to play this medley AA BB AC DD EE, repeat it, then finish with the A music. On the CD I use a type of cross picking for the quarter notes in section B, outlining the chords with a triplet feel.

Polly put the Kettle On

© 2010 Gregory Doc Rossi

La Cardeuse & Le Triomphe

© 2010 Gregory Doc Rossi

Jockey to the Fair dates from the 18th century. It comes in several versions and is found in England as a Morris dance as well as in Ireland. It sits well on the cittern as a solo piece, especially if you hold on to the chords to create the suspensions so often found in baroque music. I've teamed it up with a couple of English jigs. The Flaxley Green Dance dates from about the same period, and is associated with fiddler and wheelwright William Henry Robinson from the village of Abbots Bromley, which, like Flaxley Green, is in Staffordshire. Tom Jones was very popular in the 18th century, appearing in several mid-century tune books after the publication of Henry Fielding's famous novel. It's normally played in D, but I've set it in G to make the best use of the chords available in that key.

Jockey to the Fair

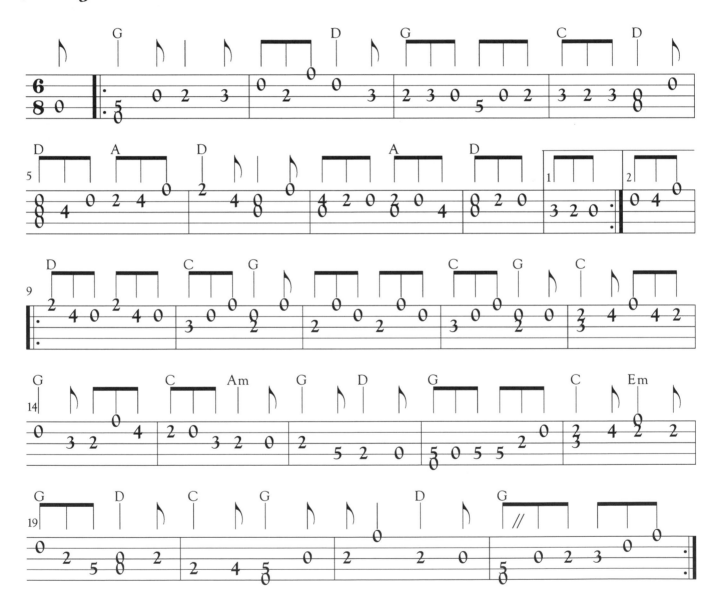

© 2010 Gregory Doc Rossi

The Flaxley Green Dance

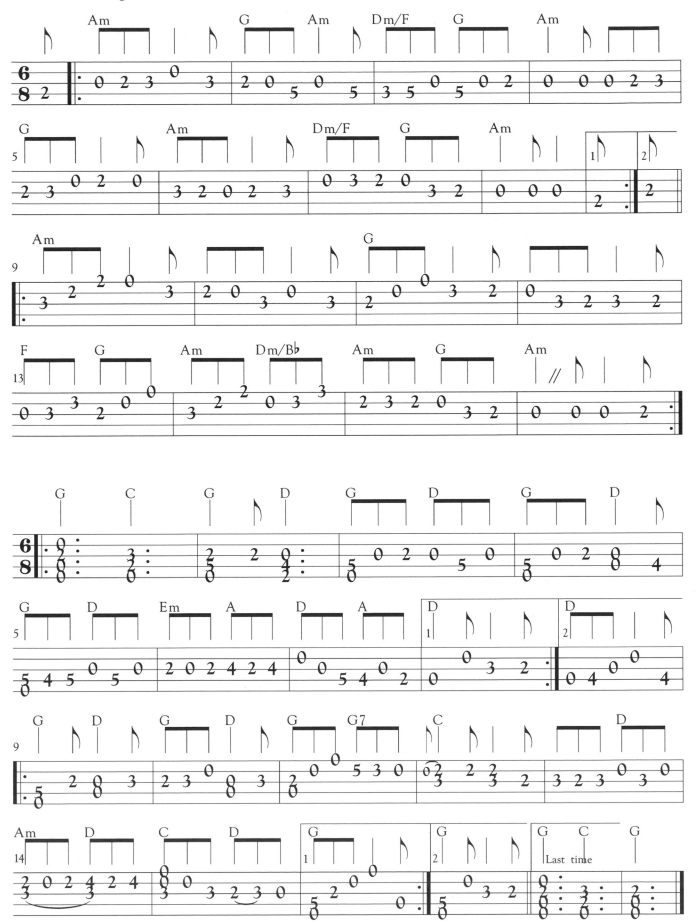

39

Foul Weather Call

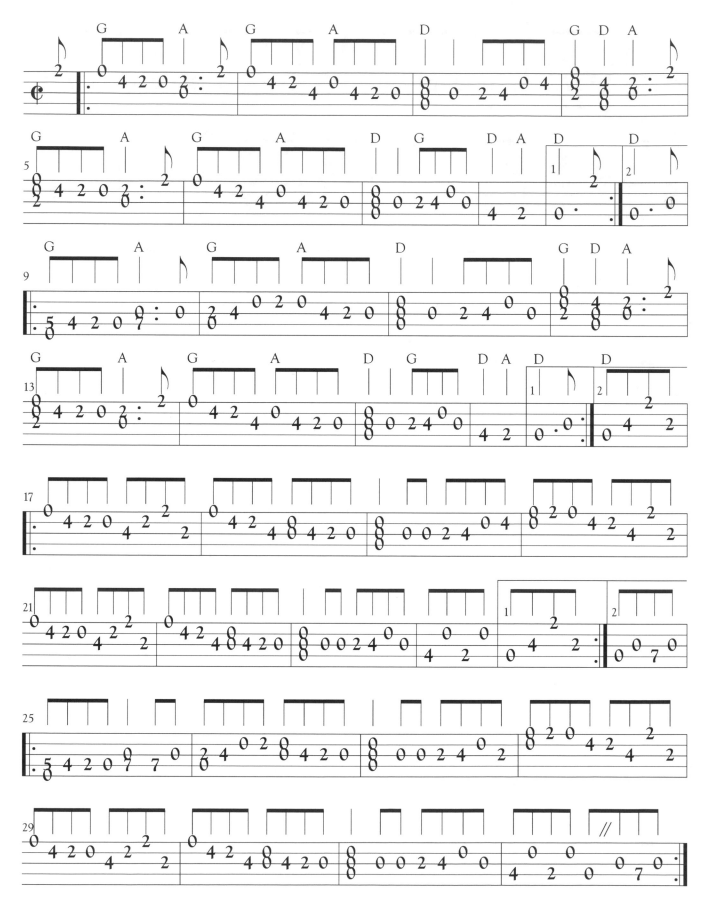

The Dorsetshire Hornpipe

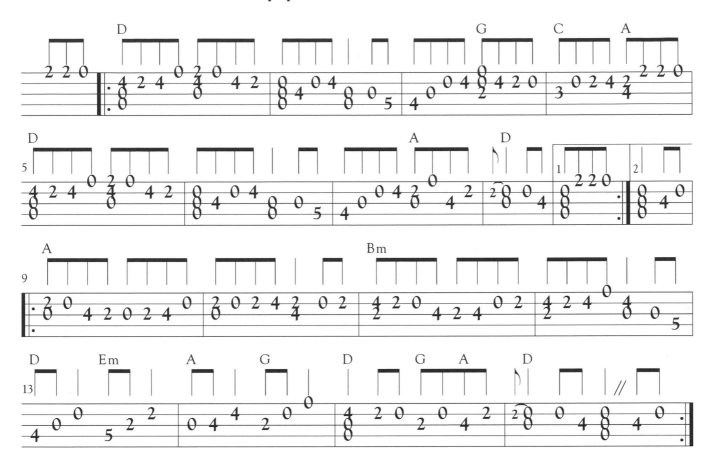

Foul Weather Call and The Dorsetshire Hornpipe are English tunes that I play as Schottisches. I learned Foul Weather Call from Dan Quinn - a really fine melodeon player - and Roger Digby. The first time through is pretty much the basic melody; the second time I develop a way of self-accompanying the tune. I often play this with right-hand damping. I may well have learned The Dorsetshire Hornpipe from Dan and Roger, too - or maybe from that grand institution of trad, Osmosis.

We finish with three duets. The first is my arrangement of a four-part jig from *Cent Contredanses en Rond*, by Robert Daubat, published in Ghent, Belgium in 1757. Daubat's fascinating collection is almost like a missing link between baroque and traditional music.

Mantovana is a very old tune that may come from the Italian city of Mantova, but I learned it in French sessions. I've written a second part to go with it. There is a barre in measure 15 at the fifth fret.

Girandula is a traditional Corsican tune usually played in Gm, so capo at the fifth fret if you find yourself in a Corsican session. You can also play it in Gm in this tuning, but I prefer it in Dm for the drones. As with Mantovana, I have provided a harmony part. The order is AA BB CC AA.

Le Concert ou La Sabatine

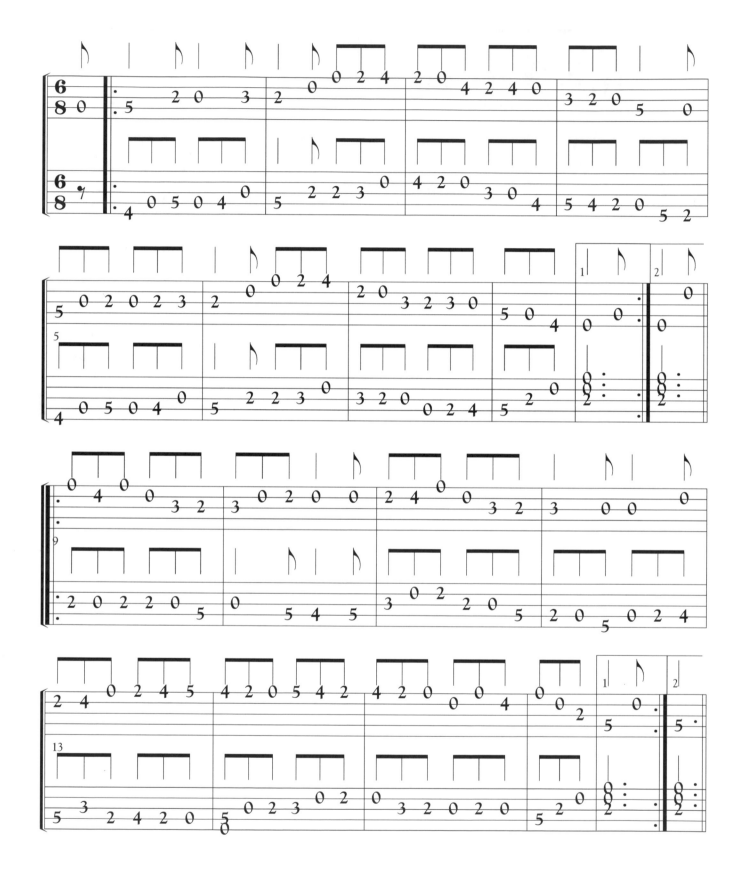

© 2010 Gregory Doc Rossi

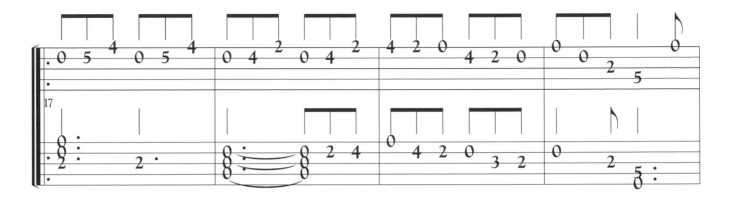

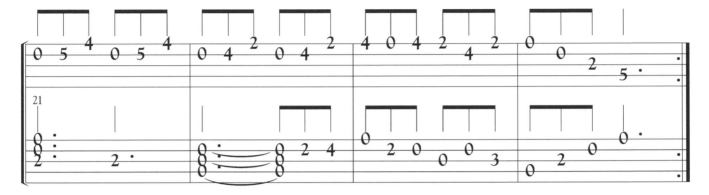

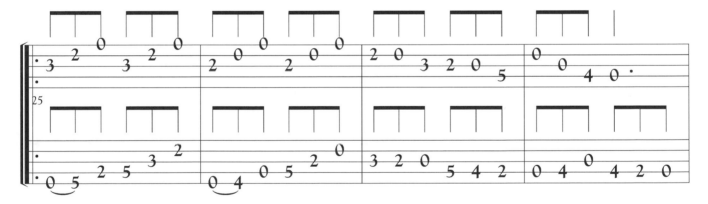

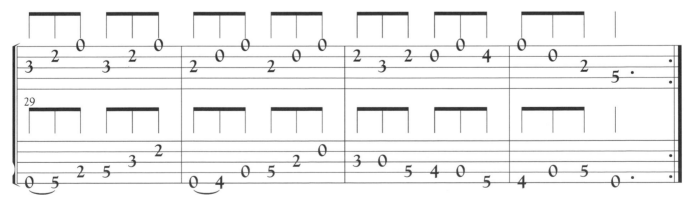

Mantovana

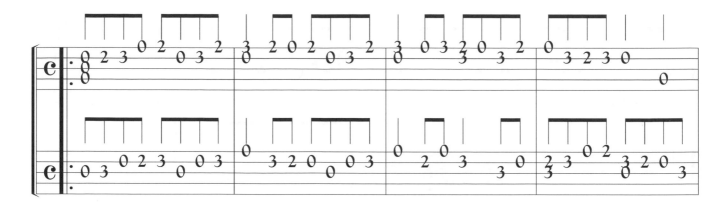

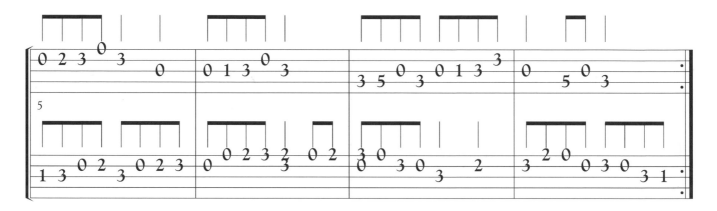

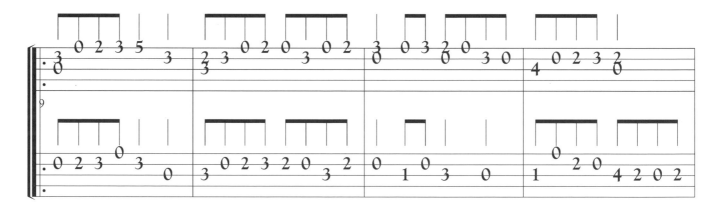

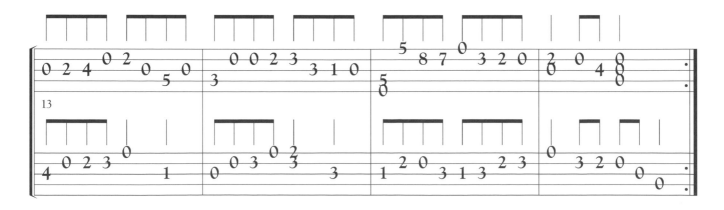

© 2010 Gregory Doc Rossi

Girandula

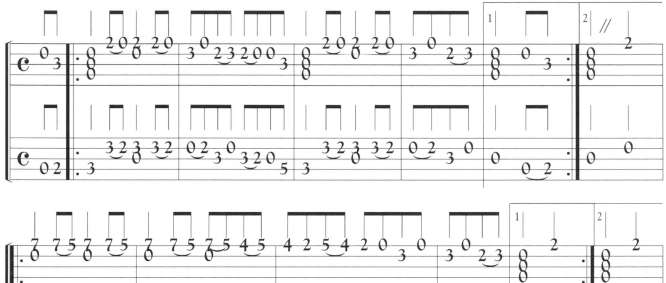

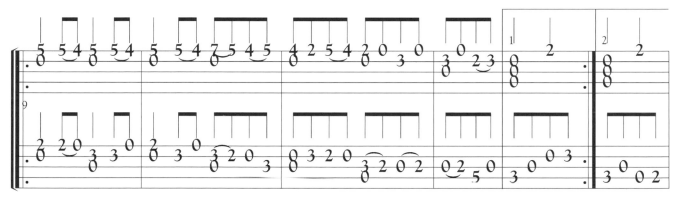

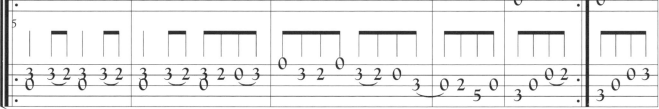

© 2010 Gregory Doc Rossi

Corsican maestro Migheli Raffaelli with a cetera built by Christian Magdeleine

45

The Peacock's Feather

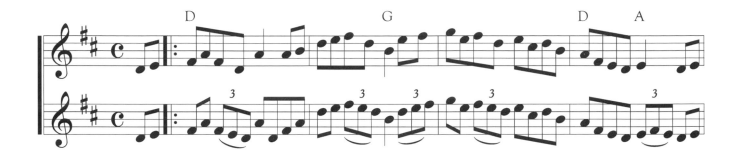

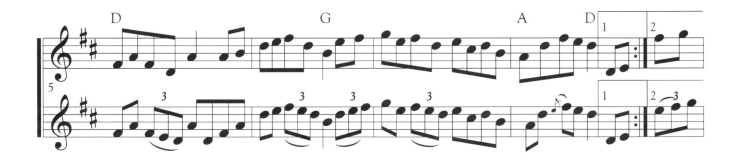

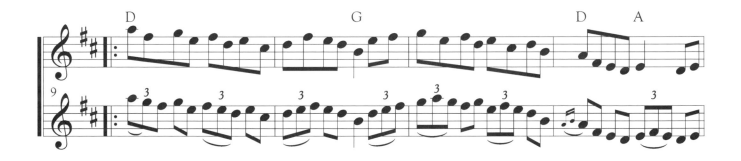

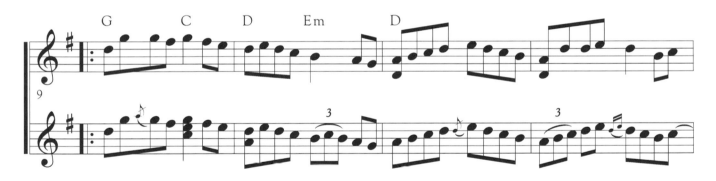

The Long Note

Rodney's Glory

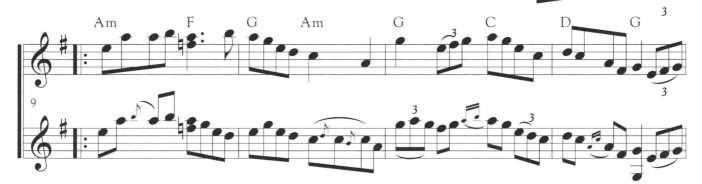

The Cordal jig

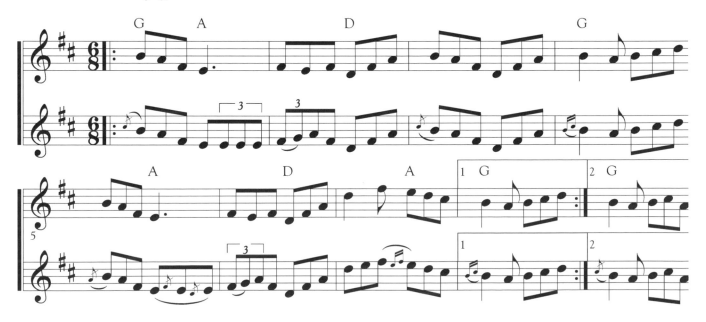

*Portuguese maestro Pedro Caldeira Cabral playing a
Coimbra-stlye guitarra*

*The Bouzouki Brothers!
Andy Irvine & Dónal Lunny*

*Swedish maestro Ale Möller with his
mandola featuring quarter-tone frets,
pin capos and an extended bass.*

Jigs

A Trip to Athlone

The Mist Covered Mountain

The Mooncoin Jig

The Lark in the Morning

The Swallow Tail Jig

The Banks of Lough Gowna

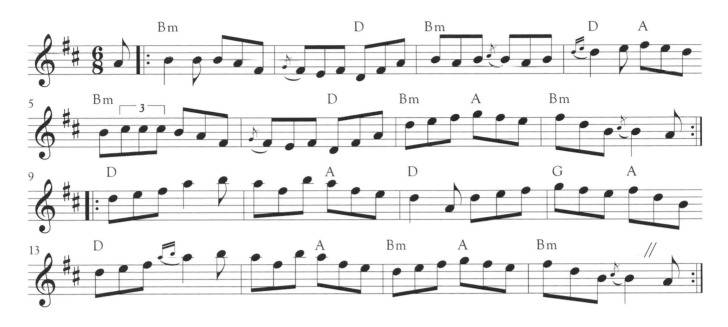

An Phis Fhliuch

Hornpipes & Set Dances

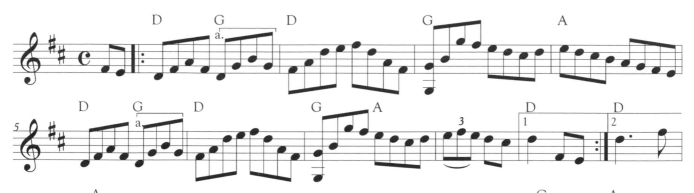

The Galway

The Greencastle Hornpipe

Alternate B music

The Liverpool Hornpipe

The Princess Royal

58

Poll Ha'penny

The Blackbird

A copy of a Renaissance cittern with diatonic fretting by Malcolm Prior

Reels

The Flowers of Edinburgh

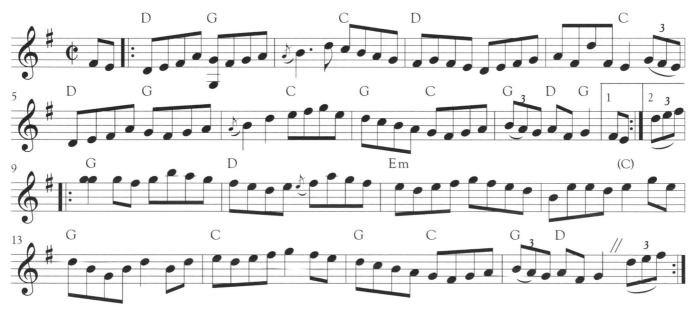

The Flowers of Michigan

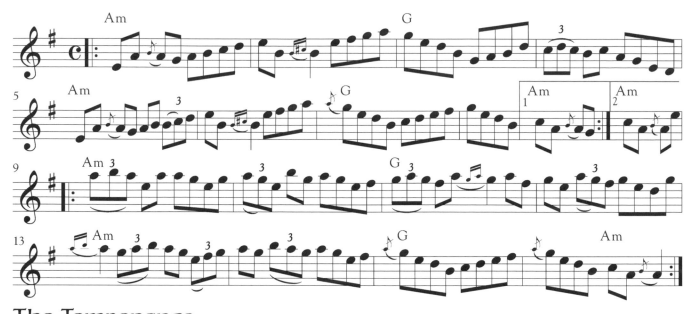

The Temperance

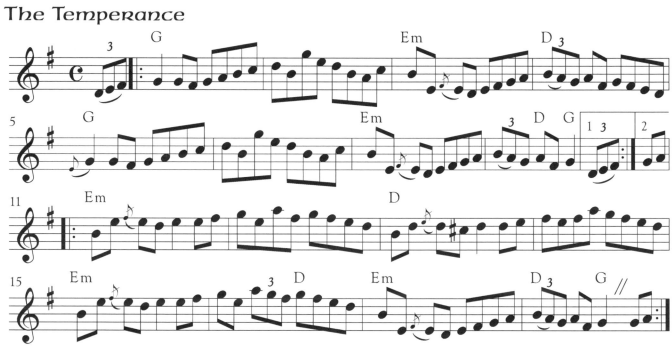

Two German citterns - a 17th-century Hamburg bell cittern by Joachim Tielke and a deluxe model Böhm waldzither, c. 1920

A guittar or cetra by William Gibson of Dublin, 1761,
and Joseph Sobol playing his 18th-century Simpson guittar

The Woman of the House

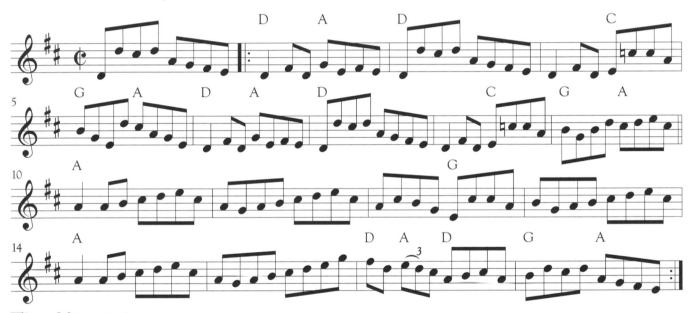

The Virginia

63

The Log Cabin

The Traveler's

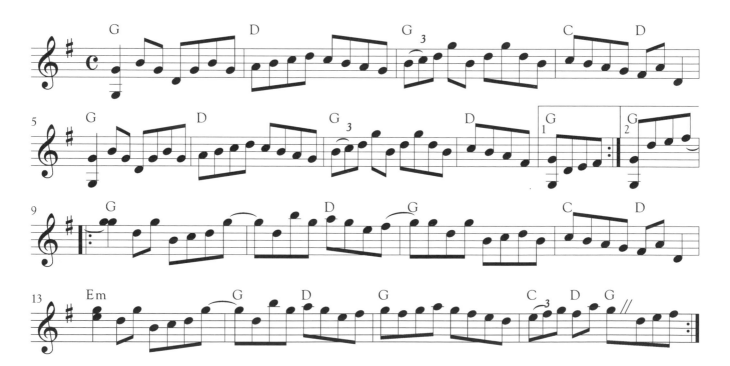

The Scholar

Alternate B music

Miss Thorton's

Alternate fingering for B music

Other Tunes

La Cardeuse & Le Triomphe

Polly Put the Kettle On

Jockey to the Fair

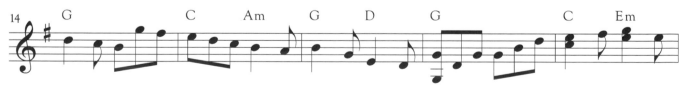

The Flaxley Green Dance

Tom Jones

Foul Weather Call

The Dorsetshire Hornpipe

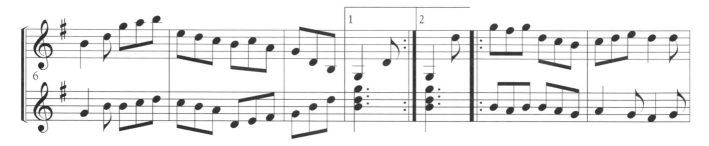

Mantovana

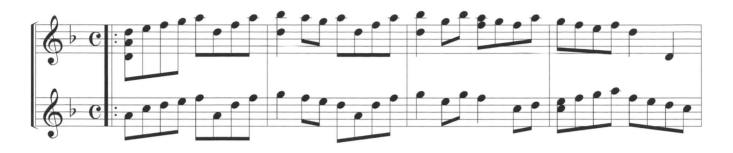

A small 18th-century guittar or cetra next to a Gibson A-style mandolin for comparison

Girandula

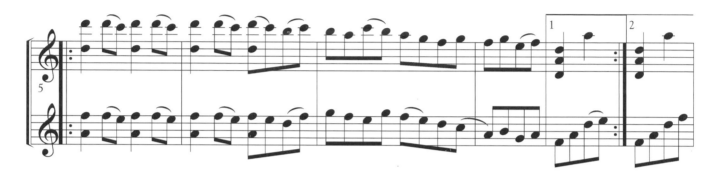

An 18th-century Corsican cetera from Bastia (right) and a cetera based on an instrument from Merusaglia, by Ugo Casalonga

II. Common Chords in G D A D G Tuning

 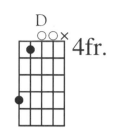 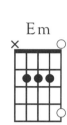 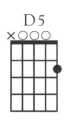

 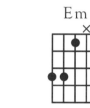 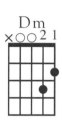 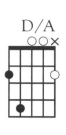 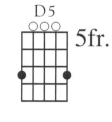 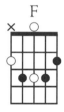 

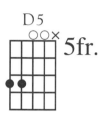 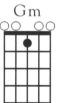 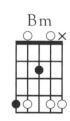 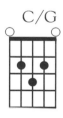

 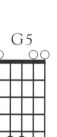  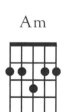 

D   D 4fr.   D/A   D5

D5 5fr.   D5 5fr.   Dm   Em

Em   Em 7fr.   F   F/C

G   G   G5   Gm

A   A5   Am   Bm

C   C   C   C/G

III. Cd Tracks

The tunes are played at a medium tempo. I never play a tune the same way twice, but I have tried my best to play as closely as possible to these arrangements. For the pieces in Part One, the basic version is followed by the ornamented version. For the rest of the pieces, variations are played in the repeated sections; for example, A1 is the basic version, A2 is ornamented. Although the tunes are arranged into sets, each tune is played individually.

1. The Peacock's Feather basic version
2. The Peacock's Feather with ornaments
3. The Fairies' Hornpipe basic version
4. The Fairies' Hornpipe with ornaments
5. The Long Note basic version
6. The Long Note with ornaments
7. The Humours of Kilcogher basic version
8. The Humours of Kilcogher with ornaments
9. The Cordal Jig basic version
10. The Cordal Jig with ornaments
11. Rodney's Glory basic version
12. Rodney's Glory with ornaments
13. Brian O'Lynn
14. A Trip to Athlone
15. The Mist Covered Mountain
16. The Mooncoin Jig
17. The Lark in the Morning
18. An Phis Fhliuch
19. The Swallow Tail Jig
20. The Banks of Lough Gowna
21. Poll Ha'penny
22. The Cliff
23. The Galway
24. The Greencastle
25. The Greencastle Alternate B
26. The Liverpool Hornpipe
27. The Princess Royal
28. The Blackbird

29. The Flowers of Edinburgh
30. The Flowers of Michigan
31. The Temperance Reel
32. Woman of the House
33. Virginia
34. The Log Cabin
35. The Traveler's Reel
36. The Scholar
37. The Scholar Alternate B
38. Miss Thorton's
39. Miss Thorton's Alternate B
40. Polly Put the Kettle On
41. La Cardeuse & Le Triomphe
42. La Cardeuse & Le Triomphe Alternate B
43. Jockey to the Fair
44. The Flaxley Green Dance
45. Tom Jones
46. Foul Weather Call
47. The Dorsetshire Hornpipe
48. Le Concert ou La Sabatine Melody
49. Le Concert ou La Sabatine Harmony
50. Le Concert ou La Sabatine Duet
51. The Mantovana Melody
52. The Mantovana Harmony
53. The Mantovana Duet
54. Girandula Melody
55. Girandula Harmony
56. Girandula Duet

A Note to Guitarists

You can play all of the tunes in this book on the guitar by tuning C F C G C F, low to high, and putting a capo at the second fret. The lowest line in the tablature then corresponds to the fifth string.

More Great Guitar Books from Centerstream...

SCALES & MODES IN THE BEGINNING
INCLUDES TAB
by Ron Middlebrook
The most comprehensive and complete scale book written especially for the guitar. Chapers include: Fretboard Visualization • Scale Terminology • Scales and Modes • and a Scale to Chord Guide.
00000010..$11.95

FINGERSTYLE GUITAR
INCLUDES TAB
by Ken Perlman
Teaches beginning or advanced guitarists how to master the basic musical skills of fingerpicking techniques needed to play folk, blues, fiddle tunes or ragtime on guitar.
00000081 Book Only.................................$24.95

POWER RHYTHM GUITAR
by Ron Middlebrook
with Dave Celentano
This book/CD pack features 31 lessons for rhythm guitar that you can play by yourself, in a band, or as a back-up musician. Includes full band examples in many musical styles, including basic rock, country, hard rock, heavy metal, reggae, blues, funk, and more.
00000113 Book/CD Pack............................$19.95

THE FLATPICKER'S GUIDE
INCLUDES TAB
by Dan Crary
This instruction/method book for flatpicking teaches how to play accompaniments, cross-picking, and how to play lick strums. Examples in the book are explained on the accompanying CD. The CD also allows the player to play along with the songs in the book.
00000231 Book/CD Pack.........................$19.95

ACOUSTIC BLUES GUITAR
INCLUDES TAB DVD
by Kenny Sultan
This book/CD pack for intermediate-level players incorporates slide or bottleneck playing in both open and standard tunings. All songs are primarily fingerstyle with a monotone bass used for most.
00000157 Book/CD Pack............................$18.95
00000336 DVD $19.95

GUITAR CHORDS PLUS
INCLUDES TAB
by Ron Middlebrook
A comprehensive study of normal and extended chords, tuning, keys, transposing, capo use, and more. Includes over 500 helpful photos and diagrams, a key to guitar symbols, and a glossary of guitar terms.
00000011..$11.95

BLUES GUITAR
INCLUDES TAB
by Kenny Sultan
Through instructional text and actual songs, the author covers blues in five different keys and positions. Covers fingerstyle blues, specific techniques, open tuning, and bottleneck guitar. The CD includes all songs and examples, most played at slow speed and at regular tempo.
00000283 Book/CD Pack............................$17.95

ARRANGING FOR OPEN GUITAR TUNINGS
INCLUDES TAB DVD
By Dorian Michael
This book/CD pack teaches intermediate-level guitarists how to choose an appropriate tuning for a song, develop an arrangement, and solve any problems that may arise while turning a melody into a guitar piece to play and enjoy.
00000313 Book/CD Pack $19.95

BLUES GUITAR LEGENDS
INCLUDES TAB DVD
by Kenny Sultan
This book/CD pack allows you to explore the styles of Lightnin' Hopkins, Blind Blake, Mississippi John Hurt, Blind Boy Fuller, and Big Bill Broonzy. Through Sultan's arrangements, you will learn how studying the masters can help you develop your own style.
00000181 Book/CD Pack............................$19.95
00000193 DVD $19.95

FLYING FINGERS
INCLUDES TAB
by Dave Celentano
This book/CD pack offers clear demos of techniques proven to increase speed, precision and dexterity. 32 examples cover arpeggios, different picking techniques, melodic sequences, and more. The CD demonstrates each technique at three speeds: slow, medium and fast.
00000103 Book/CD Pack...........................$15.95

P.O. Box 17878 - Anaheim Hills, CA 92817
(714) 779-9390   www.centerstream-usa.com

More Great Guitar Books from Centerstream...

JAZZ GUITAR SOLOS BY GEORGE PORTS AND FRANK SIBLEY

Jazz horn players are some of the best improvisers ever. Now guitarists can learn their tricks! This book features 12 solos (progressing in difficulty) from jazz saxophonists and trumpeters transcribed in easy-to-read guitar tab. The CD features each solo played twice, at slow and regular tempo.
00000188 Book/CD Pack...$19.95

LATIN STYLES FOR GUITAR

by Brian Chambouleyron
A dozen intermediate to advanced originals in notes & tab display various Latin American styles. For each, the CD features the lead part as well as an accompaniment-only rhythm track for play along.
00001123 Book/CD Pack $19.95

THE PATRIOTIC GUITARIST

arranged by Larry McCabe
This red, white and cool collection contains 22 all-American guitar solos for fingerpickers and flatpickers. Includes: America the Beautiful • The Battle Hymn of the Republic • The Marines' Hymn • The Star Spangled Banner • Yankee Doodle • and many more patriotic favorites. The accompanying CD includes demo tracks for all the tunes.
00000293 Book/CD Pack......................................$19.95

GUITAR TUNING FOR THE COMPLETE MUSICAL IDIOT

by Ron Middlebrook
There's nothing more distracting than hearing a musician play out of tune. This user-friendly book/DVD pack teaches various methods for tuning guitars – even 12-strings! – and basses, including a section on using electronic tuning devices. Also covers intonation, picks, changing strings, and much more!
00000002 Book/DVD Pack..$16.95
00001198 DVD $10.00

ASAP CLASSICAL GUITAR

Learn How to Play the Classical Way
by James Douglas Esmond
Teacher-friendly or for self-study, this book/CD pack for beginning to intermediate guitarists features classical pieces and exercises presented progressively in notes and tab, with each explained thoroughly and performed on the accompanying CD. A great way to learn to play ASAP!
00001202 Book/CD Pack $15.95

THE GUITAR CHORD SHAPES OF CHARLIE CHRISTIAN

by Joe Weidlich
Chord shapes are moveable; thus one can play the riffs in virtually any key without difficulty by simply moving the shape, and fingerings used to play them, up or down the fingerboard. The author shows how the chord shapes – F, D and A – are formed, then can easily be modified to major, minor, dominant seventh and diminished seventh chord voicings. The identifiable "sound" of a particular lick is preserved regardless of how many notes are added on either side of it, e.g., pickup notes or tag endings. Many examples are shown and played on the CD of how this basic concept was used by Charlie Christian.
00000388 Book/CD Pack $19.95

THE COUNTRY GUITAR STYLE OF CHARLIE MONROE

Based on the 1936-1938 Bluebird Recordings by The Monroe Brothers
by Joseph Weidlich
This great overview of Charlie Monroe's unique guitar performance style (he used just his thumb and index finger) presents 52 songs, with an in-depth look at the backup patterns & techniques from each chord family (G, F, D, C, E, A), plus special note sequences, common substitutions and stock backup phrases. Includes the bluegrass classics "Roll in My Sweet Baby's Arms," "My Long Journey Home" and "Roll On, Buddy," plus a discography and complete Bluebird recording session info.
00001305 ....$19.99

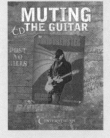

MUTING THE GUITAR

by David Brewster
This book/CD pack teaches guitarists how to effectively mute anything! Author David Brewster covers three types of muting in detail: frethand, pickhand, and both hands. He provides 65 examples in the book, and 70 tracks on the accompanying CD.
00001199 Book/CD Pack...$19.99

HYMNS AND SPIRITUALS FOR FINGERSTYLE GUITAR

by James Douglas Esmond
Originating in the South during the antebellum days on the old plantations, at religious revivals and at camp meetings, hymns and spirituals are the native folk songs of our own America. This collection features 13 songs, some with two arrangements – one easy, the second more difficult. Songs include: Were You There? • Steal Away • Amazing Grace • Every Time I Feel the Spirit • Wade in the Water • and more.
00001183 Book/CD Pack $19.95
00001177 DVD $19.95

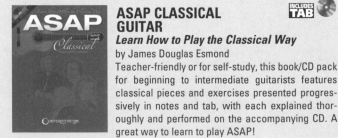

P.O. Box 17878 - Anaheim Hills, CA 92817
(714) 779-9390   www.centerstream-usa.com